GREEN MAN

This series features unsolved mysteries, urban legends, and other curious stories. Each creepy, shocking, or befuddling book focuses on what people believe and hear. True or not? That's for you to decide!

45th Parallel Press

Published in the United States of America by Cherry Lake Publishing
Ann Arbor, Michigan
www.cherrylakepublishing.com

Reading Adviser: Marla Conn MS, Ed., Literacy specialist, Read-Ability, Inc.
Book Designer: Felicia Macheske

Photo Credits: © Aleshyn_Andrei/Shutterstock.com, cover; © SpeedKingz/Shutterstock.com, 5; © kryzhov/Shutterstock.com, 7; © Max kegfire/Shutterstock.com, 9; © aleramo/Shutterstock.com, 10; © Susan Quinland-Stringer/Shutterstock.com, 13; © Dundanim/Shutterstock.com, 13; © Collin Quinn Lomax/Shutterstock.com, 15 © Liderina/Shutterstock.com, 16; © Africa Studio/Shutterstock.com, 18; © Oleg Golovnev/Shutterstock.com, 21; © Steve Pepple/Shutterstock.com, 22; © frankie's/Shutterstock.com, 24; © Savo Ilic/Shutterstock.com, 27; © ESB Professional/Shutterstock.com, 29

Graphic Elements Throughout: © iofoto/Shutterstock.com; © COLCU/Shutterstock.com; © spacedrone808/Shutterstock.com; © rf.vector.stock/Shutterstock.com; © donatas1205/Shutterstock.com; © cluckva/Shutterstock.com; © Eky Studio/Shutterstock.com

45th Parallel Press is an imprint of Cherry Lake Publishing.

Library of Congress Cataloging-in-Publication Data has been filed and is available at catalog.loc.gov

Cherry Lake Publishing would like to acknowledge the work of The Partnership for 21st Century Skills.
Please visit *www.p21.org* for more information.

Printed in the United States of America
Corporate Graphics

TABLE OF CONTENTS

Chapter One

BEWARE OF THE GREEN MAN

What kinds of stories are there about Green Man? Why is Green Man green?

Teens should be careful. They shouldn't be out late at night. They shouldn't be on dark roads. They shouldn't talk to strangers. But some teens don't listen. They break the rules. They put themselves in danger. Green Man will get them.

People can see Green Man coming. He has green skin. He has a green glow. The glow is all around him. No one knows why he's green.

Some people blame **aliens**. Aliens are beings from space. They took Green Man. He turned green in space.

Parents told Green Man stories to keep their children safe at home.

CONSIDER THE EVIDENCE

There's another story about green people. They're called the "green children of Woolpit". Woolpit is in England. There were two children. They were brother and sister. They had green skin. They lived in the 12th century. They spoke their own language. They wore strange clothes. They only ate green beans. They got lost. They showed up in Woolpit. A man adopted them. The children eventually ate other foods. They lost their green skin color. They got baptized. Then, the boy got sick. He died. The girl learned to speak English. She said they came from Saint Martin's Land. This is a world where green people lived.

Some people blame nature. Lightning hit Green Man. He didn't die. He was in shock. He turned green. He became crazy. He lived in a tunnel. He scared people.

Some people blame science. Green Man is **radioactive**. This is strong energy. It causes **deformities**. Deformities are when body parts don't form correctly. Some think a power line fell on him. This burned off his face. This made his skin green.

Some people blame green shirts. Green Man wore a green **plaid** shirt. Plaid is a pattern. This shirt was his favorite. Green Man wore all green. The color seeped into his skin. His skin became green.

People made up scary stories about Green Man.

Chapter Two

CHARLIE NO-FACE

What is the Green Man legend? What does Green Man look like?

Green Man is also known as Charlie No-Face. His story started in the 1950s. It started in western Pennsylvania. There are many stories about him. This is one of the stories.

Two teens want to go for a drive. Their parents are worried. They tell them about a faceless man. The man has green skin. He roams dark roads. He looks for **prey**.

Prey means victims. The parents say, "If you go out after dark, Charlie No-Face may grab you."

The teens go at night. They drive to a dark tunnel. They want to see if Green Man is real.

Pennsylvania teens have heard Green Man stories most of their lives.

Green Man must be called.

They enter the tunnel. It's dark. They can't see anything. They wait. Nothing happens. The boy beeps his horn. He does this twice. They yell, "Charlie No-Face!" Then, they see something. They see a blurry light. The light gets closer. It gets greener. They see a shadow. The teens see a man. They scream.

Green Man's face is deformed. His nose, mouth, and eyes are melted together. He has a hole in his cheek. The hole has teeth. Green Man's nose is a hole in his skin. His eyes are covered over. They look like two puffy areas of skin. They twitch. It looks like he's blinking.

SPOTLIGHT
BIOGRAPHY

Elizabeth Sweetheart is called the Green Lady of Brooklyn. She only wears green. She wears different shades of green. She wears green from head to toe. She's been doing this for over 20 years. She started with homemade green nail polish. She added a bright green streak in her hair. Next, she wore green clothes. Then, she worked on her house. She bought green furniture. Everything she buys is green. She loves green. She said, "It's the most positive color in the whole world. It makes me feel happy." She also does it to make others happy. Kids call her "Miss Green."

Green Man hides in the tunnel. He knows he's ugly. He doesn't want people to see him. He hates people with faces. He's jealous.

He goes to the car. The teens drive away. They don't let him touch their car. People say that Green Man has a charge. If he touches their car, the car will explode. This would kill the teens. Their ghosts would be stuck with Green Man. They were scared that Green Man would steal their faces. Green Man puts these faces over his face.

Green Man may be green with envy.

Chapter Three

IT'S NOT EASY BEING GREEN

Who is Raymond Robinson? What happened to him?

Raymond Robinson was born on October 29, 1910. He was born in Beaver County, Pennsylvania. He was called Ray. He had a normal childhood. That changed on June 18, 1919. He had a bad accident.

He was playing with friends. He saw a bird's nest. It was on an electric pole. It was by a tunnel. Robinson and his friends dared each other. The dare was to climb the pole. Robinson did it. He climbed. He touched a power line. The power line was dangerous. He got shocked. It sent 22,000 **volts** into his body. Volts are units of electricity. This melted his face off.

Robinson and his friends were heading to a swimming hole.

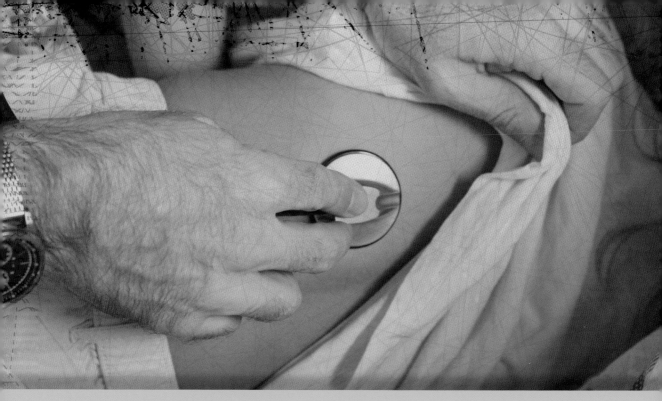

Robinson spent a lot of time with doctors. But he was very friendly.

Robinson burned his upper chest. He lost both eyes. He lost one ear. He lost his nose. He lost an arm below the elbow. His mouth was deformed. His skin turned green. This was from the shock. He got a sickness. He didn't heal correctly.

Everyone thought Robinson would die. But he lived. He was in the hospital for a long time. He had many operations. Doctors took flaps of skin. They sewed the flaps over the holes where his eyes and nose used to be.

He stayed positive. He was a good man. His nephew said, "He never complained about anything."

REAL-WORLD
CONNECTION

Professor Tomas Egana is a scientist. He works at the Institute of Biological Engineering. He's at the Catholic University of Chile. He created green skin. He used micro-algae. Algae are sea plants. Micro-algae are super tiny. Scientists call the skin "hulk." (It's because the Incredible Hulk is green.) Artificial skin is tricky. Artificial means fake. It can't make oxygen. Plants create oxygen. This is important. Oxygen lets the micro-algae skin be used in transplants. It can be used to help wounds. It can live in bodies. The algae die in about 10 days. This is enough time for skin to become part of the body. The green color will fade.

Robinson worked from home.

Robinson stayed home. His family took care of him. He listened to the radio. He made doormats. He made wallets. He made belts.

He got a fake nose. He got fake glasses. He liked taking long walks. He used a walking stick. He kept one foot on the path. He kept the other foot off of it. He walked a trail near his house. But a coal company destroyed it. So, he walked on a highway. He did this late at night.

He died on June 11, 1985. He was 74 years old. He died from old age.

Chapter Four

A TALE OF TWO MEN

How did Raymond Robinson become an urban legend? How did people treat him? How are Green Man and Robinson different?

Robinson was famous for his nightly walks. Drivers saw him. They were curious. They thought he looked like a ghost. They started spreading stories. They talked about a green ghost with no face. People went to see for themselves. This was in the 1950s.

Stories about him spread. People added details. Not all these details were true. Robinson became an **urban legend**. Urban legends are modern folktales.

There are two stories. One is Robinson's story. The other is Green Man's story. Robinson was a good man. Green Man is evil. People like Green Man's story more. It's more fun. Robinson's story is sad.

Urban legends warn against modern dangers and fears.

People didn't treat Robinson well. They were scared of him. Children screamed when they saw him. People said mean things to him. They called him names.

A man delivered groceries to Robinson's house. He saw Robinson. He said, "I dropped the boxes and ran."

A woman walked past him on the road. She said, "I was so scared. It was unreal."

There was a market by Robinson's road. People went to the market. They said a monster was on the road. They wanted to call the cops.

People hunted Robinson. (Green Man hunted others.)

INVESTIGATION TIPS

- Visit Green Man Tunnel. Stay in the car. Keep the car running. Don't stop. Don't park. Don't go at night.

- Talk to people who live in Pittsburgh. Ask them if they know about Green Man.

- Go to the library. Learn more about urban legends. Learn more about Raymond Robinson. Learn more about Green Man stories.

- Read local newspapers from Pittsburgh. Check out the crime reports.

- Look for green glows. Be aware at all times.

- Get a map of Pittsburgh. Study it. Know your way around town. Know the major highways.

Robinson walked the highways at night. People thought this was spooky.

Robinson avoided people. He knew what he looked like. He didn't want to upset others. He didn't go out in public. He didn't go out in the daytime.

This is why he walked at night. He covered himself in darkness. He hid from cars. He could hear cars coming. He hid behind trees. He hid behind bushes.

But some people were nice to him. They gave him gifts. They learned more about him. They learned his story. They learned he was a nice guy. Robinson took pictures with them.

Chapter Five

GREEN MAN TUNNEL

What is Green Man Tunnel? What happens at the tunnel?

Robinson and Green Man are two different men. Robinson would never hurt anyone. Green Man is scary. But Green Man Tunnel is scarier. Many teens go there. They think it's haunted. They look for Green Man. They get in their cars. They go to the tunnel. They turn off the lights. They yell, "Charlie No-Face!" Some say they see him in the darkness.

Many locations could be Green Man Tunnel. But the most popular is in Pittsburgh. Pittsburgh is in western Pennsylvania. Green Man Tunnel is an old train bridge. It was built in 1924. It was the Piney Fork Tunnel. It serviced coal mines.

Green Man Tunnel is where Piney Fork River empties into Peters Creek.

EXPLAINED BY SCIENCE

Hypochromic anemia is also called green sickness. It's when red blood cells are less red than normal. Red blood cells become paler. They can't access iron in the blood. So, iron builds in the liver. Hypochromic anemia causes skin to turn green. It creates green patches. These patches show up on different areas of the body. It makes people tired. It causes shortness of breath. It causes headaches. It slows growth. It makes people less hungry. There are many causes of hypochromic anemia. People may have low iron. They may have other sicknesses. They may be taking drugs. They may have lead poisoning.

Piney Fork Tunnel was **abandoned** in 1962. This means the tunnel is no longer used. It's covered in **graffiti**. Graffiti is painting on public buildings. It's against the law. **Locals** are people living in the town. They say the tunnel is spooky.

Some people like to play **pranks**. Pranks are jokes. Some people pretend to be Green Man. They wear a costume. They wait for teens to come to the tunnel. They peek in their car windows. They scare teens. This could explain some **sightings**. Sightings are reports that Green Man exists.

Real or not? It doesn't matter. The Green Man lives in people's imaginations.

Green Man's story is most popular in Pennsylvania. But it has spread to other states.

DID YOU KNOW?

A witness met Raymond Robinson. He said he wasn't green. Robinson wore green shirts. His green shirts reflected off car headlights. This made him look green.

Some people called Raymond Robinson a zombie.

Raymond Robinson is buried in Grandview Cemetery. His plot overlooks the tunnel where he was injured.

Green Man Tunnel is popular on Friday nights after football games. Sometimes, cops have to go there. They control traffic. They ticket anyone who stops at the tunnel.

Some say they've seen Green Man blow cigarette smoke out of the hole in his cheek.

Local men from Pittsburgh fought in the Vietnam War. They took pictures of themselves with Raymond Robinson. They took these pictures to war. This is one way the Green Man legend spread.

People would go to Raymond Robinson's house. They'd honk their horns. They'd yell, "We want to see Charlie!"

A carnival owner wanted to hire Raymond Robinson for his "freak show."

CONSIDER THIS!

Take a Position: Read the 45th Parallel Press book about Bunny Man Bridge. Compare and contrast these stories. Which urban legend is better? Argue your point with reasons and evidence.

Say What? Explain how Green Man and Raymond Robinson are connected. Explain how people treat them. Explain why they are treated differently. Explain why people like Green Man's story more than Robinson's story.

Think About It! Green Man is believed to have worn green shirts. Elizabeth Sweetheart likes to wear green clothes. Imagine wearing only one color. Which color would that be? Why?

LEARN MORE

- Brunvand, Jan Harold. *Encyclopedia of Urban Legends*. Santa Barbara, CA: ABC-CLIO, 2001.

- Holt, David. *Spiders in the Hairdo: Modern Urban Legends*. Little Rock, AR: August House, 1999.

- Peterson, Megan C. *Haunting Urban Legends*. North Mankato, MN: Capstone Press, 2014.

GLOSSARY

abandoned (uh-BAN-duhnd) no longer used

aliens (AY-lee-uhnz) beings from outer space

deformities (dih-FORM-ih-teez) features that aren't developed correctly; defects

graffiti (gruh-FEE-tee) the illegal painting or defacing of public buildings

locals (LOH-kuhlz) people who live in a town

plaid (PLAD) pattern that is a crisscross

pranks (PRANGKS) jokes

prey (PRAY) victims

radioactive (ray-dee-oh-AK-tiv) having bad energy that could be poisonous

sightings (SITE-ingz) reports of seeing something or someone

urban legend (UR-buhn LEJ-uhnd) modern folktale

volts (VOHLTS) units of electricity

INDEX

ABOUT THE AUTHOR

Dr. Virginia Loh-Hagan is an author, university professor, former classroom teacher, and curriculum designer. She used to work at the University of Pittsburgh. She didn't visit the Green Man Tunnel. She lives in San Diego with her very tall husband and very naughty dogs. To learn more about her, visit www.virginialoh.com.